Thoughts from the Thirteenth Floor

Reflections on God, the Bible, and Other Matters of Faith

ADAM RIVEIRO

Copyright © 2016 Adam Riveiro

All rights reserved.

All Bible verses are from the King James Bible
ISBN: 1530597943
ISBN-13: 978-1530597949

CONTENTS

Introduction

INTRODUCTION

Almost immediately after Liberty Baptist Church in Easton, MA opened in June of 2013, I was given the opportunity to write a monthly column in our town's newspaper, the *Easton Journal*. Each month, it's a joy to sit in front of my computer and write these pieces for the people of our town. This book is a compilation of many of those columns. It's my prayer that these short chapters will encourage and strengthen you on your spiritual journey.

1 *The Bible: Our Method of Growth*

For each new year that our church has been open, I have prayerfully chosen a theme for the year. The reasoning behind this is to give us a biblical point of emphasis to consider for the entire twelve months. In 2015, our theme was "That Ye May Grow." This is taken directly from 1 Peter 2:2, which says, "As newborn babes, desire the sincere milk of the word, that ye may grow thereby."

Why these four simple words? It's my desire that our church is continually excited about digging deep into the Word of God. According to 1 Peter 2:2, we are to desire the Word so that we can grow in our Christian lives. Over the years, I have found that many Christians think of the Bible much like Miracle-Gro. The purpose of putting this special food on your plants is to give them an extra boost. Nobody would attempt to have a plant live on fertilizer alone because without light and water the plant cannot be fruitful.

The Bible, however, is not like Miracle-Gro. It is not an extra "add-on" to our daily lives; it is our daily sustenance. Job said in Job 23:12 that "I have esteemed the words of his mouth more than my necessary food." Jesus, who Himself is called the Word (John 1:1), said in Matthew 4:4, "It is written, man shall not live by bread alone, but by every word that proceedeth out of the mouth of God." When we neglect to study the Word of God daily, we end up starving ourselves of the nutrients He has stored up for us.

Why do we need this daily infusion of the Bible?

Because the Bible helps us grow in so many different ways. Consider what Paul penned in 2 Timothy 3:16, "All scripture is given by inspiration of God, and is profitable for doctrine, for reproof, for correction, for instruction in righteousness." The Bible tells us what's right (doctrine), what's wrong (reproof), how to get our lives right (correction), and how to keep our lives right (instruction in righteousness). Consider these as the four food groups for a Christian to maintain a balanced scriptural diet.

The next verse in 2 Timothy tells us that, by utilizing the Word, "the man of God may be perfect, throughly furnished unto all good works." Paul is emphasizing to us that we can take comfort in the Bible as our sole authority for everything in our lives. There is no other book, no tradition, or dogma that can supersede it (2 Peter 1:19,20). What a blessing to the Christian that all we need for our Christian life is contained in the precious Word of God!

2 *You've Got Mail*

Remember the joys of letter writing? I mean good, old-fashioned letter writing. There was something special about hand-writing a letter, putting it in the mail, and waiting for a response. When you got a reply, you hurriedly pulled it out of the envelope and read the contents. Usually, depending on who the letter was from, you'd read it several times over.

Remember how great that was? The honest answer is: probably not. With the advent of email and Facebook, electronic communication has replaced letter-writing as our primary mode of communication with family and friends. Let's be honest, it's fantastic to have the ability to correspond with our family and friends instantly through the power of the internet. But, I think you'd also agree that as a culture we've lost something special now that the art of writing a letter by hand has gone the way of the Pony Express.

The reason for me saying this is because, a couple of months ago, I received a handwritten letter in the mail from a family friend whom I hadn't heard from in a long time. This man was like a grandfather to me, so you can imagine the joy that I felt when I inspected the envelope. Quickly, I opened it and began to read several pages of news, stories, and encouragement that he sent me. Honestly, I forgot how good it felt to get a real, honest-to-goodness letter! A few days later, it felt equally as good to write a letter back to him.

Have you ever considered that the Word of God is the Lord's personal letter to you? The Bible was inspired by the Spirit of God (2 Timothy 3:16) and written for our benefit. God wrote this beautiful letter and sent it to us so that we can read its good news, true stories, and encouragement over and over again. It's not just a book for the entire world, but it's a book that God intended for you personally. In fact, Jesus Christ Himself said in Matthew 4:4 that you and I need this letter, "Man shall not live by bread alone, but by every word that proceedeth out of the mouth of God." It's a personal letter that each of us needs to read, study, and love.

From Genesis 1 to Revelation 22, each word in the Scriptures is there for a particular purpose. God wants us to study His Word so that we can understand what truth is (2 Timothy 2:15). Truth brings life. Truth brings joy. Truth brings freedom (John 8:32). We don't read the Bible simply out of duty or habit. Much like someone who is eagerly anticipating a letter in the mail from a dear friend, we read the Bible with delight and a spirit of anticipation.

So when you look at a Bible, don't think "return to sender." Pick it up and read it with gladness. It's God's beautiful letter, written just for you.

3 *A Lesson From the Snow*

Note: After 2015's historic snowfall of over 110" in a season, I decided to write this column.

Let me start by telling you that I was born and raised in Florida. We moved to this area almost two years ago to start Liberty Baptist Church. I love living in New England. I love living in the Boston area. Specifically, I love living in Easton. So, please understand that what I'm about to say isn't a complaint; it's more of an observation.

I'm ready for the snow to melt. It's wreaked havoc on our mailboxes, driveways, homes, and cars. It's mocked our normal schedules and routines. It brought the subways and trains to a virtual standstill. The good news is that spring is rapidly approaching, and with spring comes thawing. I think we can all agree, no matter what your theology is, that it's time for the snow to melt.

I know that I'm not the only one who feels this way. Many people who have lived in this area their entire lives feel the same way. Many of our church members have expressed the same attitude to me as well. We're ready for it to just...go...away.

However, before it does, I want to dwell on an object lesson from the Bible using snow as an illustration. Isaiah 1:18 says, "Come now, and let us reason together, saith the LORD: Though your sins be as scarlet, they shall be as white as snow; Though they be red like crimson, they shall be as wool." Romans 3:10 tells us that none are righteous (right before God). If this is the case, one could wonder if there is any hope for mankind. Thank God, however, the verse in Isaiah tells us that there is a way for our sinful soul to become as white as the snow. This way is not achieved by performing good works, for Titus 3:5 says it's "Not by works of righteousness which we have done, but according to his mercy he saved us…" In fact, good works have never throughout human history saved a person's soul. It is only by God's mercy, extended to us through the blood of Christ that anyone can be born again (Romans 5:9). Jesus made this point clear in John 3:17 when he said, "For God sent not his Son into the world to condemn the world; but that the world through him might be saved."

Although we get very tired of snow, especially as it gets dirty in the days following a storm, the freshly fallen snow is a wonderful reminder of God's mercy to us. When the snow makes us weary, we can rejoice in the lesson God gives us in each snowflake.

4 *Don't Look Back! Press On!*

Have you ever heard of John Landy? Probably not, but for a few short months in 1954, he was the fastest man in the world. The Aussie broke the world record for the mile run and garnered great accolades for the achievement.

In August of the same year, Landy met Roger Bannister, the previous world record holder for the mile, in a race that was hailed as "The Race of the Century." The world tuned in with great anticipation; over 100 million people listened to the radio and millions more watched on the still-new invention of television. No doubt, it was a contest for the ages, but probably not in the way that you would expect.

Heading into the final lap of the race, Landy held the lead. But, as he pressed towards the finish line, he couldn't help but wonder how far Bannister trailed behind him. Against his better judgment, he quickly looked over his shoulder. This one motion was just enough to slow his stride, allowing Roger Bannister to overtake him and claim the victory. Later, when John Landy spoke to a reporter from Time Magazine, he said, "I would have won the race if I hadn't looked back."

Several times in the New Testament, our lives are compared to a race. In Philippians 3:13-14, Paul states, "Brethren, I count not myself to have apprehended: but this one thing I do, forgetting those things which are behind, and reaching forth unto those things which are before, I press toward the mark for the prize of the high calling of God in Christ Jesus."

Paul pressed toward the mark (think of the mark as the

finish line) for the prize of the high calling of Jesus Christ. He could only do this, by his own admission, by forgetting those things that were behind him. What were those things? Paul explains this in great detail earlier in the chapter, but I believe Hebrews 12:1 summarizes it well when the author says "...let us lay aside every weight, and the sin which doth so easily beset us, and let us run with patience the race that is set before us." Things from our past that hold us back and sin, in particular, should be laid aside so that we can run the race God has before us. Are you in bondage to sin or to painful experiences in your past? Christ invites us to lay those aside and look ahead to Him.

It's important to note that when Paul says in Philippians 3:14 that we have a high calling, the word "high" in the Greek gives the connotation that the calling is so high, it's heavenly. We can only obtain this high calling of Jesus Christ by first making Him our Savior and asking Him to forgive us of those sins that so easily beset us. So, friend, don't look back. Press on!

5 Barnabas: The Son of Consolation

Have you ever noticed that at the end of a game show, the folks who don't win are offered "consolation prizes?" Usually, these prizes are something like a set of dishes or a CD player. When the contestants receive these consolation prizes, they don't usually look too thrilled because they really wanted to win a Caribbean cruise or a new car instead. But, since they lost the game, they have to go home with their meager consolation winnings.

When I think of the word "consolation," my mind is drawn to these small prizes that are supposed to make people that lose gameshows feel better. So, when we find in Acts 4:36 that a man named Joses was nicknamed Barnabas, which means a "son of consolation," we may not immediately think that such a title is a compliment. However, very few people in the Scriptures were given a more complementary title than Barnabas. In the early days of Christianity, Barnabas was a man who went out of his way to be a help to those around him. We can learn several important traits from his life:

• **Generosity:** We find at the end of Acts 4 that there were people in the church who had great needs. The Roman government offered no assistance to families or individuals who were not citizens. The Bible tells us that Barnabas sold a piece of land and gave the proceeds of the sale to the church so that it could be disbursed to the people who needed it the most.

• **Forgiveness:** In Acts 9, many of the believers in Jerusalem were doubtful that Saul of Tarsus had really accepted Christ. Before his salvation experience, Saul had dedicated his life to eradicating those who followed Christ. You can imagine why so many would be hesitant to now welcome Saul with open arms into their church. However, Barnabas was the first to extend a hand of fellowship and forgiveness towards Saul. Because of this, others soon followed suit. This man named Saul later used the name Paul, who we know as the great apostle.

• **Mentorship:** When the church at Antioch was established in Acts 11, Barnabas moved from his home in Jerusalem to help these young Christians. Acts 11:23 tells us that "...when he came, and had seen the grace of God, was glad, and exhorted them all, that with purpose of heart they would cleave unto the Lord." In fact, verse 26 tells us that he stayed in Antioch for a year to teach and encourage the brethren.

Although Barnabas may not be one of the most well-known figures in the Bible, his example is a reminder to us that we must look beyond our own needs and see the needs of others. Have you considered that someone may need your generosity, forgiveness, or biblical mentorship? Give it freely and without reservation. This is the true meaning of being a son (or daughter!) of consolation.

6 *Is God On My Side?*

Have you ever asked yourself if God is on your side? Maybe, you were making a big, life-changing decision. It could be that you were going through a season of life where things just were not going the way that you wanted them to go. No matter the reason, this is a question that sometimes goes through our mind. However, as understandable as this line of thinking is, it misses a much greater point that we should consider.

In Joshua 5, Joshua was surveying Jericho when he came face-to-face with the Lord. God's sword was drawn and He was standing on the road blocking Joshua's route. Joshua, who was startled and not completely aware of who he was facing, asked a very natural question: "Art thou for us, or for our adversaries?" God answered this question in an unusual way. He simply answered, "nay." At first glance, this doesn't seem to be a proper answer to a question where the only answers should have been "I'm with Israel" or "I'm with Jericho."

However, when we consider the nature of who God is, this is the perfect answer to Joshua's question. God refused to choose between Israel and Jericho, which was why He answered "no" to a question that was not a "yes" or "no" question. He loves all people and does not choose sides in the same way that we often do.

The principle for us here is that, instead of asking if God is on our side in life, *we should ask, "am I on God's side?"*. Hebrews 13:8 states that Jesus Christ is the same "yesterday, and today, and forever." One of the glorious characteristics of God is that He is immutable, meaning that he is both unchanging and unable to be changed. Because of this, we must align our lives and way of thinking to what He has for us, not the other way around.

This type of thinking makes some people uncomfortable. In fact, there are those who even mock living this way as dangerous or weak-minded. However, I can promise you that there is no better way for a Christian to live. One of my favorite passages of Scripture is Proverbs 3:5,6, which says, "Trust in the LORD with all thine heart; And lean not unto thine own understanding. In all thy ways acknowledge him, And he shall direct thy paths." By placing our trust in God and His ways, we know that He will lead us down the correct paths of life. What an encouragement!

7 *The Biblical Recipe For Peace*

Wouldn't you like to experience peace? In this crazy world that we live in, we can all at least agree on one thing: we'd like a little bit of peace in our lives. Although peace sometimes seems elusive, the Bible gives us a recipe for peace in Philippians 4:6,7: "Be careful [anxious] for nothing; but in every thing by prayer and supplication with thanksgiving let your requests be made known unto God. And the peace of God, which passeth all understanding, shall keep your hearts and minds through Christ Jesus."

These two verses give us a recipe for experiencing the peace of God in our lives. The recipe calls for four distinct ingredients:

•**Prevailing Prayer:** Paul tells us in verse six that everything should be done in prayer. I often find myself taking big things to God in prayer-- things I know I can't do myself. However, there are so many matters each day that I neglect to bring before the Lord. Then, I find myself fretting over them later. Joseph Scriven, in the famous hymn "What a Friend We Have in Jesus," puts it this way: "Oh, what peace we often forfeit, oh, what needless pain we bear, all because we do not carry everything to God in prayer!"

•**Selfless Supplication:** The word "supplication" means to bring forth a petition. When used in conjunction with prayer, as it is in Philippians 4:6, supplication gives the connotation of petitioning on behalf of someone else. So, when we pray, we must not only pray for ourselves. We must also petition God on behalf of the needs of others. By praying for peace in someone else's life, we are closer to experiencing peace ourselves.

● **Giving of Gratitude**: Paul reminds us that when we pray and offer supplications, we must do it with the spirit of thanksgiving. When we are troubled in our spirits, we often can't find anything to be thankful for. Take some time and think upon all of the blessings that you experience in life. Ephesians 5:20 tells us to be "giving thanks always for all things unto God and the Father in the name of our Lord Jesus Christ."

● **The Right Recipient:** To experience the peace of God, our requests must be made known unto God. Of course, we understand that He already knows all of our needs. But, he wants to hear us speak them to Him. What an awesome privilege we have, to pray to God our Father!

When we use all four of the ingredients that are found in Philippians 4:6, we can experience "the peace of God, which passeth all understanding" If you are anxious, worried, or troubled, why don't you use this biblical recipe and enjoy a batch of peace today?

It is well-known in our church that I am not mechanically inclined. I am so thankful that we have many who work well with their hands and can create, fix, and repair. That's a wonderful thing, but unfortunately, I never acquired those skills. This is especially true when it comes to cars. Would you believe that I just tried to change my blinker fluid last week? Well, maybe I'm not that limited in my knowledge, but I'm close!

As little as I know of cars, my understanding of horse-drawn carriages is even more limited. However, I heard a pastor recently relate the spiritual life of a child of God to a wagon wheel. It was so simple, even someone with little mechanical knowledge could understand. Yet, it was so profound that it really made me stop and think about my own life. This pastor said, "God is not merely a spoke in the wheel, rather, He is the hub around which all of life revolves."

What a thought! We can be so busy in our lives, that often without realizing it, God just becomes "something else" in our lives-- He becomes just another spoke. If we aren't careful, we can have the spokes of family, work, school, and other responsibilities along with God. Please understand, I am not saying any of those things are bad, in fact, they are all good and necessary things. However, we can allow God to become just another "thing" in our lives. When that happens, He ends up revolving around us, which is a backward way to live. This is why Jesus said in the Sermon on the Mount to "...seek ye first the kingdom of God, and his righteousness; and all these things shall be added unto you" (Matt. 6:33).

In our lives, do we put God first in all that we do? Do we allow Him to be the hub and let all the other parts of our lives revolve around Him? Some may ask, "If God is the central focus of a person's life, won't they have less time for their family, job, and friends?" I submit to you that it's quite the opposite. The more we make God the center of our lives the more we will become better spouses, better employees, and better friends. By making God the hub, all of the spokes start to revolve in the proper direction causing everything to work in a cohesive unit.

1 Corinthians 10:31 reminds us that "Whether therefore ye eat, or drink, or whatsoever ye do, do all to the glory of God." Our first and primary responsibility as Christians is to give God glory in all areas of our lives. When we do that, everything else in our daily walk will move in sync. You don't have to know much about mechanics to understand that! Now, if you'll excuse me, I'm going to go top off my blinker fluid.

9 *Caricatures of the Church*

Have you ever been to a theme park or the fair and seen artists drawing caricatures? Caricature artists are experts at taking one feature and exaggerating it to the point of silliness. If your nose is a bit larger than the norm, you can expect it to fill half of the page. Do you have a toothy grin? You can expect it to take up most of your face. These pictures are funny to look at, but no one really believes that they are an accurate representation of reality. There's a big difference between the drawings of a caricature artist and a police sketch artist. One purposely misrepresents the subject, while the other strives for accuracy and detail.

I've found that many people have created caricatures of what church is like. No, these are not physical drawings that they have made, but instead, they are skewed pictures that they have created in their minds. Usually, these caricatures come from a small kernel of truth but have been blown up so large that they are nowhere near reality. In the past, people have made statements to me such as, "All any church cares about is money," or "churches are made up of a bunch of hypocrites." More than likely, there was an incident that happened in that person's life that caused them to think this way. However, allowing a bad experience to permanently change your thinking of church and the Bible is nothing more than creating a caricature in your mind. It's taking a small thing and blowing it up so large that the accurate image is forgotten.

Without a doubt, no church is perfect, including ours! But, to focus on a small negative, instead of seeing the entire picture of what a Bible-preaching church is leads to false assumptions. 2 Corinthians 10:5 encourages us to "Cast[ing] down imaginations, and every high thing that exalteth itself against the knowledge of God, and bring[ing] into captivity every thought to the obedience of Christ." This means that we should not allow false ideas, particularly about God, to color our thinking. Rather, we should bring our thoughts under Christ's control. After all, He reminded us in John 14:6 that He is truth.

Have you been living with a caricature of the church? Why don't you take some time this Sunday to visit God's house and sketch a new picture of what it is all about? Don't miss what God has for your life!

10 *A Church Full of Addicts*

Did you know the Bible tells us that we are to be addicts? I am speaking of 1 Corinthians 16:15, which says, "I beseech you, brethren, (ye know the house of Stephanas, that it is the firstfruits of Achaia, and that they have addicted themselves to the ministry of the saints)."

When the apostle Paul writes of being an addict, he means that we should be addicted to the ministry. Paul references to the household of Stephanas in this verse. No one can be quite sure who Stephanas was because the Bible does not speak of him outside of the epistle of 1 Corinthians. Some believe that he was the Philippian jailer who cried out to Paul in Acts 16, "What must I do to be saved?" No matter who he was, one thing we can be sure of: this fellow was a man who made it his business to be a servant to others.

When we hear the word "addict," the mental picture is usually not a good one. Addiction to drugs, alcohol, and other sinful activities are devastating behaviors to behold. When one is addicted to something, they are at the mercy of that activity. However, Paul uses the word "addiction" in a positive light. He tells us that we are to be totally and unashamedly "hooked" on meeting the needs of those around us.

Often times, people use the word "minister" to explain the role of a pastor. No doubt, it is the primary job of a pastor to be a servant, even while leading. But by the same token, all those who are Christians are called to be servants. Christ, our ultimate example, was said to have taken the form of a servant (Philippians 2:7). In the same way, 1 Peter 4:10 tells us that we are to be ministers of the manifold (abundant) grace of God.

Can you imagine what would happen to a church if everyone made a point to be addicted to the ministry? What would our churches and communities be like if, instead of looking to be blessed, we look for ways to be a blessing. To be the type of servant God wants us to be, we can't just be casual, part-time ministers of the grace of God. Rather, being a servant of God should consume our thoughts and actions. Let's purpose in our hearts to serve God in a greater way, not to obtain salvation or favor with God (Titus 3:5), but out of our love and devotion to Him and to those around us.

I remember some time ago, our family was in a hospital waiting room in Florida. My mom was having surgery to remove some cancerous masses from her abdomen, and there was a large amount of our extended family waiting with us. If you've ever had to wait hours on end for a loved one's surgery, you know the minutes go by very slowly. To pass the time, someone found a puzzle and laid it on the table in front of us. We were pretty desperate for a diversion, so we eagerly opened the box and dumped out the hundred or so pieces.

After several minutes, we figured out that something was wrong with the puzzle. It just wasn't coming together like it should have. In desperation, someone inspected the box again and saw something we had all missed. With a black marker, someone had scribbled on the box "MISSING PIECES." I wish we had seen that before we wasted our time trying to put the puzzle together!

As a pastor, I often get to talk to folks who are looking for a church to attend. Of course, there are several important factors to consider. Jesus said in John 4:24 "they that worship Him [God] must worship him in spirit and in truth." This means that when finding a church, it's important to seek a place that has a right demeanor (spirit) and that faithfully preaches and teaches from the Bible (truth). Although no church is perfect, its people should strive to be right in these two areas.

However, there is one aspect of the process of finding a church that is often neglected. Instead of trying to find the perfect church, have you considered that *you are perfect for a church?* God desires each person who is born again to be part of a local church (Hebrews 10:25; Acts 2:41). We also see from 1 Corinthians. 12:12-13 that each church functions much like a body and each individual as one of its parts: "For as the body is one, and hath many members, and all the members of that one body, being many, are one body: so also is Christ. For by one Spirit we are all baptized into one body."

Paul continues in 1 Corinthians 12 saying that when one part of the human body is gone, it makes it much more difficult for the body to function as a whole. In the same way, when a person is missing from a church, it makes it much more difficult for the church to function. It's like a puzzle that doesn't have all of the pieces. It leads to frustration.

Have you considered that you are the piece that's missing from a church? In your quest for a church that worships both in spirit and truth, make sure you seek God for direction. No doubt, He will lead you to the church that is "missing pieces." There, you can be a perfect fit.

12 Fellowship: More Than a Bucket of Chicken

I have great memories from growing up of church potlucks and socials. A normal church potluck had all types of delicious entrees and desserts. Plus, since I was raised in the South, no church potluck was complete without someone bringing a bucket of fried chicken and a gallon or two of sweet iced tea— extra sweet, please!. Usually, these post-church activities were called "fellowships." Although I know each denomination claims to have the best potlucks, it's my theological position that Baptists have the most delicious ones, hands down. Well, I may not be able to prove that, but it sure seems like it to me!

Now that I am a pastor, I find myself often announcing special fellowships at our church as well. Each time I announce a fellowship, the men and ladies of the church bring all sorts of goodies for us to feast on. I enjoy a good church fellowship. It's a great time for the congregation to relax around good food and conversation. As a pastor, getting to hear people talk, laugh, and let their guard down around plates of food makes me feel good.

However, even though I love the concept of fellowship in church, sometimes it's too limited to an after-church lunch. True biblical fellowship is so much more than a bucket of chicken. True fellowship in a church occurs when members share a common bond in Jesus Christ and are unified in passion and purpose for Him. We find the first example of this in Acts 2:42, when, after Pentecost, "they continued steadfastly in the apostles' doctrine and fellowship, and in breaking of bread, and in prayers." Although I believe the early church did a fair share of breaking of bread, they also continued together in fellowship. This meant that they united for the cause of Christ. The remainder of Acts 2 tells us that their fellowship compelled them to pray for each other, provide for each other, and praise God for His goodness.

Although some would suggest that a person can know Jesus Christ as their Savior and not go to church, my response would be, "Why?" Why would we want to miss out on biblical fellowship? Why would we want to pass on the opportunity to be encouraged by our fellow believers? The early church relished the opportunity to be together and the Bible tells us that they did so on a daily basis.

Although we need fellowship with others in our church, most of all, every person needs to have fellowship with Jesus Christ. Have you united your life to His eternal purpose? His plan for you is simple and is found in Philippians 3:9,10, that you might "...be found in him, not having [your] own righteousness, which is of the law, but that which is through the faith of Christ, the righteousness which is of God by faith: That [you] may know him, and the power of his resurrection, and the fellowship of his sufferings, being made conformable unto his death." That kind of fellowship is more satisfying and longer lasting than any bucket of chicken!

13 *Church: Open for Business*

A couple of years ago, our family took a vacation to Florida. As many New Englanders have experienced, the drive down I-95 is a long one (especially with three children under the age of 10, which ours were at the time). With each state that passed by, we were more excited to reach our destination: the Sunshine State. Finally, as the last miles of Georgia slipped away, we crossed the border into Florida. We made it! Everyone cheered and I honked the horn as we passed by a large sign that proclaimed, "Welcome to Florida."

As I pulled into the Florida visitor center on the way home, I noticed something on the sign that I hadn't noticed a couple of weeks before. Below the welcome message and the current governor's name was a statement I thought was interesting: "Open for Business." Apparently, the state recently added this tagline to convince visitors that Florida is a great place for businesses to grow.

I started to consider that little phrase as we continued the drive back home. My thought was this: "Open for Business" is a great motto for church. Of course, church is not a business, but churches are open to conduct very important business. In fact, before Jesus ascended into heaven, He gave His church a Great Commission to explain what our business must be: "Go ye therefore, and teach all nations, baptizing them in the name of the Father, and of the Son, and of the Holy Ghost teaching them to observe all things whatsoever I have commanded you…" (Matthew 28:19-20). It's the job of churches to tell the world the good news of the Gospel of Jesus Christ.

"What exactly is that good news?" you may ask. The good news is that although we were spiritually dead in our sins, Christ died on the cross to pay the penalty for our sins (Romans 5:8). The gift of salvation is free for all who accept it (Romans 10:9,10,13; Ephesians 2:8,9). This gift is available to all, regardless of gender, race, age, or economic status. Liberty Baptist Church's business is to let everyone know that Jesus Christ loved them so much that He was willing to die on the cross for them (1 Peter 2:24).

No doubt, churches probably shouldn't be putting "Open for Business" signs in front of their buildings. However, what a joy it is for us to be able to do the business of our Heavenly Father! I can think of no greater business or higher calling for a church to be part of.

14 *Making Church Relevant Again*

There are a lot of buzzwords in popular Christianity today. One of the most widely used ones is the word "relevant." Of course, there's good reason why people use the word. Who wants to be irrelevant? Nobody sets out in whatever they pursue with a desire to be irrelevant. We want everything that we do, whether it is by our words or our actions, to be relevant and meaningful to the people around us.

In various advertisements and magazines, I notice churches often using the word "relevant" to explain various parts of their ministry. Sometimes, you will hear phrases like "relevant Bible message" or "relevant music." Believe it or not, there is even a church in my hometown called Relevant Church! I completely understand the desire to stay relevant as a church. Would anybody want to be called Irrelevant Church? However, I think the use of the word can make people confused about a much greater point.

The greatest way for a church to stay relevant is to preach and teach from the Word of God. Some things in life are trendy, and to stay relevant they must constantly change. However, the Bible is timeless, and when churches stick close to it, they will find that they are more relevant than they could ever possibly imagine. Are you worried about life after death? 2 Timothy 3:15 tells us that the Scriptures can make us wise unto salvation. Are you hurting? Psalm 18:2 tells us that God is our Rock. Are you confused and looking for direction? Proverbs 3:5,6 tells us that if we trust in God and acknowledge Him, He will direct our paths. These verses are just a small sample of the infinite truths available in Scripture. No matter what you are going through, the Bible has relevant truth that can change your life forever. It may be an old book, but its truths are timeless and speak to our hearts even today.

So how can a church remain relevant again in today's society? Does it require that we put the Bible to the side and settle for quick, life-coaching style pep talks from our pulpits? I would submit to you that churches are truly the most relevant when they continue to boldly and lovingly preach and teach directly from the Scriptures. After all, 1 Peter 1:25 reminds us that the Word of the Lord will endure forever. If you've never experienced the relevance of God's Word in your life, this Sunday would be a great time to start.

15 *Can Truth and Love Coexist?*

Some time ago, I came across a gentleman at his house who explained his frustration to me. He had been to a few different churches over the years, and he had never experienced a church that had the proper balance. He shared with me that he had attended churches that were strong on the truths of the Bible, but that often showed an unloving, uncaring spirit. He also had been to churches where he felt loved and accepted, but where Bible truth was not regularly articulated and taught to the people. This man, in defeat said, "Is it even possible to find a church that has both truth and love?".

It's a great shame that people have been turned off by harsh Christianity. The apostle Paul reminds us in 1 Corinthians 13:2 that "And though I have the gift of prophecy, and understand all mysteries, and all knowledge; and though I have all faith, so that I could remove mountains, and have not charity (love), I am nothing." I agree with the old saying, "People don't care how much you know, until they know how much you care."

At the same time, it's important to still preach and teach the truths of God's Word. Ephesians 4:15 reminds us to, "speak[ing] the truth in love." Someone who doesn't present truth because they are afraid to offend may seem kind, but is actually doing a great disservice. Imagine that you visited the doctor and, during the checkup, the physician found that you had contracted a potentially deadly disease. However, this disease was easily curable with the correct treatment. Would you consider the doctor loving if he withheld the truth from you because he was afraid of offending you? Rather, you would be grateful for the physician who kindly explained your ailment and patiently reviewed your treatment options. If I was to water down the truth of the Bible, I believe that it would do the hearers a grave disservice. But, that doesn't give me license to be rude or hateful. After all, we all deal with trials and temptations each day. Instead, we should "Bear ye one another's burdens, and so fulfil the law of Christ." (Gal. 6:2)

Maybe you have asked yourself the question: can truth and love coexist? I believe it has always been God's intention that they do. Don't give up until you find it!

16 *Should Church be Trendy or Old-Fashioned?*

The words "trendy" and "old-fashioned" each conjure up different ideas when we hear them. Each can be positive or negative depending on how it's placed alongside other words. When it comes to clothing, being called trendy can be a compliment, but saying that clothing is old-fashioned is rarely a compliment. On the other hand, I'd much rather eat a slice of old-fashioned pecan pie over a piece of trendy pie (I wonder what a trendy pie would look like?). Depending on what word "trendy" or "old-fashioned" is linked to determines if it's a compliment or not.

Here's a question to consider: is the best type of church trendy or old-fashioned? You'll notice that some churches will describe themselves as one of these words, but never both. A church couldn't be trendy and old-fashioned at the same time. Often, trendy churches will use current music, contemporary worship styles, and new-age methodology to stay on the cutting edge. An old-fashioned church would seemingly sing hymns and conduct services in a more traditional manner.

Where do I believe our allegiance should be in this debate? Let me begin by saying that I have no desire for our church to follow many of the trends of the world. In fact, 1 John 2:15 says "Love not the world, neither the things that are in the world. If any man love the world, the love of the Father is not in him." I have observed that constantly trying to stick with the trends and staying "relevant" is a dizzying task that can never be truly fulfilled. Why? Because our culture changes all the time! I should make clear that I'm not talking about using technology like a sound system or a video screen. Rather, I'm speaking of integrating popular culture into houses of worship, which is a different thing altogether.

I would readily admit that our church may be labeled old-fashioned due to Liberty's use of traditional music and Bible preaching in worship. However, I don't refer to our church as old-fashioned, because I believe church should rise above the labels of old-fashioned or trendy. Really, the best word to explain what I desire our church to be is "timeless." As I heard one pastor say, "We're not looking to be a twenty-first-century church, we want to be a first-century church!" I can appreciate that sentiment. Not only is God unchanging (Malachi 3:6), but His Word is unchanging as well (Isaiah 40:8). Instead of wondering what century our churches slot into, shouldn't we be more concerned about if we are following the precepts and commands of Scripture? Jesus said in John 4:23 that we must worship Him "in spirit and in truth." As the Holy Spirit and the Word are unchanging and timeless, our pattern of worship should not be tied to a time period, either an old or a new one.

What's the best type of church: trendy or old-fashioned? I'll take one that stands on the timeless Word of God and serves an unchanging God. When I read the book of Acts, the Christians at that time had an unquenchable love for God, His church, and the Scriptures. Because of this, those believers accomplished great things for the Lord. That is my desire!

17 *The Importance of Biblical Preaching*

Did you know that many experts believe that the average American's attention span is only eight seconds long? Did you know that those same experts pegged the attention span of a goldfish at nine seconds? Does that surprise you? In fact, the odds are good that you won't get much farther in this chapter than this sentence.

Are you still with me? I'd hate to see you go so soon!

Although it appears as though scientists have come to a consensus about our ever-shrinking attention span, they are not as sure about its cause. Whatever the culprits are, it's an issue that can cause a problem in our churches as well. We've all heard stories of our ancestors attending church for hours on end, all while sitting on hard wooden benches. Today, it can be hard to keep folks attention in a modern church building with plush, padded pews. I've heard many different theories on how to keep people engaged while they are at church. Probably the most common idea is that we must reduce or remove preaching from our worship services if our churches are to grow.

I have a great burden that preaching retains a place of importance in our churches. The Bible makes it clear that preaching should be an important part of public worship. Paul, in his final charge to young Timothy, says in 2 Timothy 4:2, "Preach the word; be instant in season, out of season; reprove, rebuke, exhort with all longsuffering and doctrine." Preaching must be preeminent in our churches because of the vital function it plays in the life of the congregation. As a pastor gives the message, it must convict (reprove), correct (rebuke), and comfort (exhort) those who are listening. This process is one that requires patience (longsuffering) and biblical truth (doctrine), not personal opinion.

Relegating preaching to a five or ten minutes segment of a church worship service is like trying to simmer a sauce in your microwave. It's a process that can't be done quickly, and when attempted, it can be disastrous. Certainly, as a pastor, I understand that we must be respectful of people's time when we enter the pulpit. However, we can't be in such a rush that we neglect to give a well-thought out, well-constructed Bible message that will help people draw closer to Christ.

A quote that is attributed to Alexis de Tocqueville from the mid 1800's remarks that, "I sought for the greatness and genius of America in her commodious harbors and her ample rivers - and it was not there . . . in her fertile fields and boundless forests and it was not there . . . in her rich mines and her vast world commerce - and it was not there . . . in her democratic Congress and her matchless Constitution - and it was not there. Not until I went into the churches of America and heard her pulpits flame with righteousness did I understand the secret of her genius and power." I believe our nation was built on a foundation of the Word of God, proclaimed boldly through preaching. It's my desire that we never forget our past as we look to solve the problems of the future.

Are you still with me?

18 *Why Have a Revival?*

Since our church was opened, we have had several opportunities to have revival meetings. During a revival, we have several extra nights of church services and preaching. When I talk to folks who aren't familiar with Baptist churches, they often ask me why we would hold a revival meeting? To answer that question, I usually relate revival to something many of us have experienced: spring cleaning.

When we start a spring cleaning, we do extra projects around the house that we've been putting off. Cleaning out all of the closets and the basement becomes a priority. There are several spring cleaning projects that you start planning as the snow begins to melt and as winter comes to a close. It's not that you haven't cleaned your house out all winter; it's just that spring cleaning is a special time of emphasis to sweep out every last bit of dirt and clutter.

It's our desire that, during a revival meeting, each person attending can revive and rekindle their relationship with God. Just as spring cleaning involves extra attention to cleaning, a revival meeting is a time of extra emphasis on a spiritual cleaning of the heart. The Bible makes it clear that those who are born again must live holy lives. But, if we're honest with ourselves, we would have to acknowledge that we fall short of that goal every day. In fact, we find that 1 John 1:8 says, "If we say that we have no sin, we deceive ourselves, and the truth is not in us." If we think we have nothing to clean, then we are fooling ourselves.

When we admit that we need to do some cleaning in

our lives, what should we do next? 1 John 1: 9 gives the answer: "If we confess our sins, he is faithful and just to forgive us our sins, and to cleanse us from all unrighteousness." Confession of our sins directly to God is a fundamental doctrine of the Scriptures. By doing this, we can clean our hearts and restore a close relationship with the Lord.

So why have a revival meeting? Simply put, we have one to pause from the busyness of our lives and to take time to search our heart. We do not attempt to whip people up into an emotional frenzy. Rather, each of us quietly looks inward at our heart. David put it best when he said, "Search me, O God, and know my heart: try me, and know my thoughts: And see if there be any wicked way in me, and lead me in the way everlasting" (Psalm 139:23,24). Once God reveals areas of our lives to clean, we confess them to the Lord, and He forgives us.

19 *A Heritage Etched Into Stone*

Our family recently returned from a vacation in the mountains of Pigeon Forge, Tennessee. On the way home, we took the (very) indirect route so that we could stop in Washington, D.C. for a day. Our whole family loves to visit DC, so an afternoon walking around and seeing the sights seemed like a perfect way to end our family trip.

When we got to Washington, we did something we had never done before: visited the galleries of the House and the Senate. We were especially excited because the Senate was in session and we would be able to see business take place on their floor. I have to admit, I was just as excited as my kids were! Seeing the chambers on TV so many times, it seemed almost surreal that we were able to sit in the balconies of these halls.

First, we visited the House. As my eyes scanned the empty room, I noticed something quite interesting. Directly above the chair of the Speaker of the House was the inscription "In God We Trust." How did I miss this after watching so many newscasts and State of the Union addresses? I'm not sure how I did, but my heart was encouraged to see our national motto literally etched in stone for all to see. In fact, later, I found that the House of Representatives, in a rare showing of bipartisan support, reaffirmed this saying as our national motto in 2011 by a vote of 396-9 (that's 97.8% voting "yes"). How often do so many Democrats and Republicans agree on anything?

Of course, there are references to God all over Washington D.C. The Senate chambers , which we visited next, also had the inscription "In God We Trust" as well as "Annuit Coeptis" ("God has favored our undertakings"). We also saw mentions of God all over the memorials found in the National Mall. Did you know the cap of the Washington Monument, the highest point in all of Washington D.C, says "Laus Deo," meaning "Praise to God" in Latin? These are just a few of many examples of our nation's godly heritage that can be found when touring our capital city.

Locally, there are many examples of our nation's Christian heritage as well. I'd ask those who are still unsure about this issue to visit our beautiful state house in Boston, or take the drive over to Plymouth to see more of our heritage painted in frescoes and written into marble. Even in Easton, our own Rockery memorial located in the middle of downtown is inscribed with the phrase "To God Be the Glory." No doubt, if you are not from our area, you would be able to find several similar examples as well. Friends, let's not ignore our Christian heritage, literally etched into stone.

20 *Get Involved In Your Government*

Abraham Lincoln's Gettysburg Address ended with this memorable statement: "This nation, under God, shall have a new birth of freedom -- and that government of the people, by the people, for the people, shall not perish from the earth."

As Christians, these lines are of significant value. First of all, we are rightly reminded that our nation is "under God." This was the position of both our founding documents and our founding fathers. Then, the phrase "of the people, by the people, and for the people" stresses that our government is simply made up of citizens seeking to help other citizens. Our government only works when each of us play a part in the political process. Nobody should sit on the sidelines. There is work for all of us to do, whether we are elected officials or not.

Recently, on a trip to Washington DC, I was able to schedule a short meeting with my representative in Congress, Joseph Kennedy. What was my purpose for meeting Rep. Kennedy? It was simply to let him know that the people of our congregation were praying for him as he served our area. As we talked, I acknowledged that we had several political differences, but that I was still grateful for his service and had great respect for his office. We continued to talk for several minutes, and I was honored that he allowed me to pray with him before I left. He couldn't have been more cordial or inviting to me, a complete stranger.

It's very easy to be pessimistic about the state of Washington. However, we can't complain about the state of our nation and sit idly on the sidelines at the same time. It is important that each of us is informed about the issues of the day. Contact federal, state, and local leaders about issues that are important. Of course, we must make sure we are aware of election days and exercise our right to vote.

Also, as Christians, we are admonished by the Scriptures to pray for our leaders, whether we agree with the ideology of those who represent us or not. Paul tells Timothy in 1 Timothy 2:1,2: "I exhort therefore, that, first of all, supplications, prayers, intercessions, and giving of thanks, be made for all men; For kings, and for all that are in authority; that we may lead a quiet and peaceable life in all godliness and honesty."

I'm so thankful that I was able to meet Rep. Kennedy, and I look forward to greeting him again the next time he has office hours in Easton. Let's not allow disillusionment with the state of politics to keep us from investing our votes, energy, and prayers into our government and our leaders.

21 *An Empty Seat for Christmas*

This year at the Riveiro house, there's an empty seat at the table for Christmas. Recently, my mother passed away after a six-month battle with cancer. My father, wife, children and I have all been grieving over the past several weeks at her passing. She was an amazing woman whom we loved very much. Our faith has brought us comfort and strength in a dark time, but the holidays have still been difficult for us so far. At times, it feels like we're just going through the motions, doing many of the same traditions that we have always enjoyed for Thanksgiving and Christmas, but without the same festivity as before. Things just seem off. It's an odd feeling to deal with.

I know our family is not the only one in this position. Each year, countless families deal with heartbreaking situations that make the holidays difficult. For some, it's a death in the family. For others, it's a grave health issue. Still others deal with deep loneliness and depression that worsens during the holidays. Folks in these situations are often welcomed with common seasonal greetings like "Merry Christmas" and "Happy holidays." Often, these sayings don't make us merry or happy, they just serve as a reminder that there is a void in our lives.

This year, if you have an empty seat at your table or an empty place in your heart, consider this: Jesus Christ desires to have a personal relationship with you. In fact, He gave His life on the cross to pay for our sins and reconcile us to the Father. Hebrews 7:25 tells us that Jesus "is able also to save them to the uttermost that come unto God by him, seeing he ever liveth to make intercession for them."

This verse tells us that Jesus not only wants to save us, but also would like to intercede for us. This means that He desires to intervene on our behalf. When we have times of great difficulty, He comes to our aid. Jesus Himself said in Matthew 11:29,30, "Take my yoke upon you, and learn of me; for I am meek and lowly in heart: and ye shall find rest unto your souls. For my yoke is easy, and my burden is light." This doesn't mean that pain and heartache just magically disappear. However, it does mean that we can take that pain and heartache and give it to Christ, and He will bear it on our behalf. What an amazing God!

It's my prayer that during the season of Christmas as we consider the Prince of Peace, we can rest in the peace of God which passes all understanding (Philippians 4:7).

The idyllic scene of the nativity is one that is etched into the minds of many people. Mary and Joseph are smiling at little baby Jesus, who sits peacefully in the manger. Shepherds are also huddled around the baby, watching His every move. Even the animals reverently bow their heads in acknowledgment of their holy houseguest. There's only one problem with this mental image—it's not the way it happened!

I'm not trying to burst anyone's bubble by saying this. Nor am I suggesting that you throw away the nativity scene you may have displayed in your home. What I am suggesting, however, is that we take some time to consider the reality of the events surrounding the birth of the Savior. To contemplate these things does not cheapen Jesus' birth. Instead, it gives us a greater understanding and appreciation of it.

Much of what we know of the events of Christ's birth comes from Luke 2. Specifically, Luke 2:6,7 says, "And so it was, that, while they were there, the days were accomplished that she should be delivered. And she brought forth her firstborn son, and wrapped him in swaddling clothes, and laid him in a manger; because there was no room for them in the inn."

Mary would have given birth, not in a sterile environment of a modern hospital, but in an enclosed area with animals. Why would animals have been present? Because a manger is not a synonym for a crib, but rather another name for a feeding trough. So Mary, undergoing the pains and fears of childbirth, would have had her precious baby surrounded by dirty, smelly animals, who were oblivious to the miracle happening mere feet away from them. After giving birth to Him and cleaning Him, she then had to lay him in a borrowed feeding trough for His first night's sleep. Now, compare this experience with the peaceful scene of the nativity. The two pictures don't exactly match up.

So, why would I want us to consider this less-than-picture-perfect scene surrounding the birth of Jesus Christ?

It's my desire that we consider how truly humble the birth of Jesus was. Think about it: the Creator (Colossians 1:16), the Word (John 1:1), the Almighty (Revelation 1:8) came to earth in the most unassuming of surroundings. In fact, He was born in surroundings that we would never want our own children born into. Why would God do such a thing? The answer is found in Philippians 2:7,8: "But made himself of no reputation, and took upon him the form of a servant, and was made in the likeness of men: And being found in fashion as a man, he humbled himself, and became obedient unto death, even the death of the cross."

Jesus was born in simplicity, lived as a servant, and died as the Savior. He did all of this so we could be redeemed from our sins. For me, I don't want to "clean up" that scene or make it into something akin to a Norman Rockwell painting. I want to remember the raw reality of the nativity, as this perfectly reflects the beauty of our Savior. May Jesus be the center of your celebration every Christmas season!

23 *Thanksgiving and Our Christian Heritage*

If you are like me, Thanksgiving is one of your favorite holidays of the year. I have great memories of gathering around the table with family and eating until I couldn't eat another bite. Later, the kids would all go outside and throw around the football while the adults fell asleep watching a football game on TV. The thought of Thanksgiving conjures up different memories for each of us.

But through it all, let's not forget that first Thanksgiving that took place in Plymouth. For the brave pilgrims who had sailed over 3,000 miles in search of religious freedom, Thanksgiving was not simply a day of food and fun. It was an entire week dedicated to Almighty God in gratefulness for His provision during the colony's painful first year.

Since we live only 45 minutes from Plymouth, I've had many occasions to look at the monuments scattered throughout the town. As you walk around, you see many landmarks of the faith of the pilgrims. Almost directly across from Plymouth Rock is a statue called the "Memorial to the Women on the Mayflower." The statue depicts a woman holding a Bible in her right hand. The inscription on the base reads "They brought up their families in sturdy virtue and a living faith in God without which nations perish."

A few blocks away from the action on Water Street is my favorite monument in Plymouth: the Forefather's Monument. No trip to Plymouth is complete without a visit this beautiful statue. Standing over 80 feet high, the monument is rich in symbolism. The woman depicted in granite holds her finger to the sky, pointing to the heavens. The rear of the statue contains a quote from William Bradford's Of Plymouth Plantation, "Thus out of small beginnings greater things have been produced by His hand that made all things of nothing and gives being to all things that are; and as one small candle may light a thousand, so the light here kindled hath shone unto many, yea in some sort to our whole nation; let the glorious name of Jehovah have all praise."

If you've never seen either of these testimonies of our nation's Christian heritage, I encourage you to visit them. So the next time you're passing the cranberry sauce (straight from the can, of course!), meditate on the words of the psalmist, who said: "O give thanks unto the LORD, for he is good: for his mercy endureth for ever." (Ps. 107:1)

24 *Where Did Thanksgiving Go?*

I am notorious for forgetting things. If you don't believe me, just ask my wife! Over the years, I've had to create a few different systems to keep me from forgetting even some of the simplest things. But even that doesn't always work. Once, I went on a quick two-day trip to Washington D.C. Not only did I forget to pack all of my toiletries, but I also forgot to put on my glasses before I left. I didn't realize that I had forgotten them until I was on the way to catch my (very) early morning train. I wish that this was an isolated incident, but it seems like I forget far too much, especially for someone my age!

So, with my personal history of absentmindedness, I find it interesting that I seem to remember something that most of the population has forgotten. What is that, you ask? Thanksgiving! It appears the past few years, as soon as November 1st arrives, we move right into the Christmas season. Store displays are hastily built, Christmas cards are prominently placed on store shelves, and Christmas decorations abound. It just feels like Thanksgiving has become an inconvenient speed bump before December 25.

Can I take a moment to encourage you to not forget this important holiday? Although we don't find Thanksgiving Day in the Bible, the idea of taking time to thank God for His bounty is quite biblical. The old hymn writer once wrote, "Count your blessings. Name them one by one, and it will surprise you what the Lord has done." Of course, this is an extension of a biblical principle found throughout the Scriptures, like 1 Thessalonians 5:18, "In every thing give thanks: for this is the will of God in Christ Jesus concerning you." The Thanksgiving season is a wonderful time for us to remind ourselves that we are a blessed people.

Friend, in the hustle and bustle of the season that is to come, let's not forget the beautiful message of Thanksgiving. We have much to thank God for, so let's take to heart the words of the psalmist: "Give unto the LORD the glory due unto his name; Worship the LORD in the beauty of holiness (Psalm 29:2)."

25 *Thoughts From the Thirteenth Floor*

Would you live on the thirteenth floor?

Recently, my wife and I were staying in Providence for a day to celebrate our anniversary. With my dad watching the kids for us (thanks, Dad!), we checked into our hotel. As we stepped into the elevator and pushed the button for our floor, Dianne commented on something we had noticed in other buildings in the past. "Look," she said, "they don't have a thirteenth floor." Sure enough, as I looked at the long row of buttons, the floors listed on the panel went right from 12 to 14.

A few days later, I did a bit more research, and found that many high-rise buildings and hotels do not have a floor listed as "13." Because of the connotation that the number 13 is unlucky, building owners fear that guests, residents, or businesses will refuse to occupy a 13th floor. Otis Elevators estimates that 85% of buildings they service do not have a floor labeled "13." A Gallup poll taken a few years ago showed 13% of people said they would be uncomfortable on a 13th floor (13 percent? Doesn't that seem ironic? That's doubly unlucky!).

Of course, the fascinating part of all this is that, even if a building doesn't officially list a 13th floor, it still has a 13th floor. It's not like there's a gap in the building between floors 12 and 14; the floor listed as the 14th is really the 13th!

Please understand, I'm not trying to be unkind or attempting to mock anyone. Believe me, that's not my intent. I'd just like to make a comparison and give some food for thought. As a Christian, I sometimes get told that it is foolish to put my faith in God. I've been told that no one who thinks rationally can really believe that an all-knowing, all-powerful God could be in control of the universe. However, it's been my observation that everyone believes in something. Everybody has faith. The question is this: what do we put our faith in? Some people believe that certain numbers bring good or bad fortune. Some believe that the day of your birth in conjunction with the stars and planets can predict your future. Still others have "lucky" items that they believe will help them (or maybe even their favorite sports team) achieve victory.

Maybe you noticed it, but the key word in each of the last three sentences is the word "believe." *Everyone* has faith in something. Maybe you've thought that placing your faith in Jesus Christ is just plain silly. But through reading the Bible, I truly believe that there is no other conclusion that a person can come to. The enormity of the universe shows a creator—God. The intricacy of human life demonstrates the love of God. The magnificence of the earth showcases God's handiwork.

In the end, I could give a (baker's) dozen different reasons why God exists, but this is a matter that can only be accepted by faith. This is why Hebrews 11:1 tells us "faith is the substance of things hoped for, the evidence of things not seen." Ultimately, faith in Jesus Christ brings peace. (Romans 5:1). What a wonderful truth, no matter who you are, or what floor you live on!

26 *In Conclusion*

It's my prayer that these articles have been an encouragement to you. As I'm sure you understand by now, I firmly believe that everyone must come to a point in their life where they call upon Christ as their Savior. Of course, this is not just my opinion. Jesus Himself said very clearly to Nicodemus in John 3, "Ye must be born again."

Friend, has there ever been a time in your life where you put your faith in Jesus Christ, repenting of your sins? Often times, this is where people answer with a statement like, "I'm Catholic," "I go to church," or "I've been baptized." *However, those answers miss the point of the question.* The Bible teaches us that every individual must come to a point and time in their life when they trust Jesus as their Savior.

Are you confused about where you will spend eternity? The Bible tells us very clearly what we must do:

•**Understand that you are a sinner:** Romans 3:10 says, "As it is written, There is none righteous, no, not one." Later on in the chapter, Romans 3:23 tells us "For all have sinned, and come short of the glory of God." Have you ever broken one of the Ten Commandments? Lied? Cursed? Coveted? If you've sinned even once, you've transgressed God's law and must pay the price.

•**Understand the penalty for sin:** Romans 6:23 tells us that "the wages of sin is death." What does this mean? Because of our sin, we've earned (that's what a wage is) the penalty of death. That death is not simply the grave, but

51

rather an eternity in hell (Rev. 20:11-15). This penalty cannot be erased by our good works, church membership, baptism, participation in "sacraments" or any other work (Romans, 3:20; Romans 4:6; Galatians 2:16, 21; Titus 3:5-7; Ephesians 2:8,9).

• **Understand Christ paid the penalty on the cross:** Although Romans 6:23 begins by telling us that the wages of sin is death, it continues by saying, "but the gift of God is eternal life through Jesus Christ our Lord." How is this possible? Romans 5:8 says that "...God commendeth his love toward us, in that, while we were yet sinners, Christ died for us." Jesus died on the cross so that the gift of eternal life would be available to all mankind. Of course, if something is a gift, you must accept it to become yours. Would you accept the gift of salvation?

• **Call upon the Lord to be saved:** Romans 10:9,10 explains "That if thou shalt confess with thy mouth the Lord Jesus, and shalt believe in thine heart that God hath raised him from the dead, thou shalt be saved. For with the heart man believeth unto righteousness; and with the mouth confession is made unto salvation." What must we do? Call upon Christ in prayer, repenting of our sins and accepting this free gift of salvation. By doing so, our sins will be forgiven, and we will have a home in heaven.

You may ask yourself, could it really be that simple? Could Christ truly forgive me of my sins? I'll leave you with one final story.

One cold, February night, I received a phone call from

someone in our church that a family member had a newborn baby that was in critical condition in the NICU. They asked if we could go and visit the baby and her mother. Quickly, Dianne and I hopped on the train as the snow was falling and arrived in downtown Boston. As we began to talk to the baby's mother, we began to ask about her spiritual condition. We took a Bible and showed her many of the verses that I just shared with you. I'll never forget that, with tears in her eyes, she told me, "You don't understand. God can't forgive the things I've done."

What a joy it was to take her to the book of Acts, where God recounts the conversion of Saul, who would later be called Paul. I said, "If God can save Saul, who was a murderer, He can save anyone. If Christ's blood is not powerful enough to cleanse us from all sins, then He's not God." Minutes later, we were thrilled to watch this woman bow her head, confessing her sins, calling upon Christ to save her.

So what about you? Would you pray to accept Christ right now? Understand this: simply repeating a prayer will not save you. Remember that Romans 10:9 tells us that it's not just what we say with our mouth, but also what we truly believe in our heart. If you'd like, you can use this prayer to help you:

Dear Jesus, I understand that I am a sinner and need Your forgiveness. I believe that you died on the cross and rose again to save me. I repent of my sins and know that your blood alone is able to forgive me of them. I accept your free gift of salvation. Help me to have the strength to follow you now that I have this new life in Christ. Amen.

If you made this decision today, would you do me the favor of sharing it with me? I would love to rejoice with you. My email address is *pastor@mylibertybaptist.org*. If you live locally, I'd invite you to be a part of Liberty Baptist Church in Easton so that you can grow in your new faith. If you live elsewhere, I'd be glad to assist you in finding a Bible-preaching church. May God bless you as you follow Him!

Made in the USA
Las Vegas, NV
11 February 2022

43760215R00036